Tyrone Power: The Life and Legacy of One of Hollywood's Most Famous Swashbucklers

By Charles River Editors

About Charles River Editors

Charles River Editors is a boutique digital publishing company, specializing in bringing history back to life with educational and engaging books on a wide range of topics. Keep up to date with our new and free offerings with this 5 second sign up on our weekly mailing list, and visit Our Kindle Author Page to see other recently published Kindle titles.

We make these books for you and always want to know our readers' opinions, so we encourage you to leave reviews and look forward to publishing new and exciting titles each week.

Introduction

A lobby card featuring Bankhead in *Faithless*

"Tyrone Power was the god of my adolescence. I would return to see his pictures over and over again. I would go first thing in the morning and stay through the last showing at night." – Sophia Loren

Hollywood has never lacked leading men who could captivate viewers with dramatic performances that depict them as suave romantics or dashing heroes, especially during the Golden Age of Hollywood, when stars like Humphrey Bogart,

Clark Gable, and Cary Grant graced screens. But in the mid-20th century, one of the most popular stars was a man who's been frequently overlooked.

At the time, the studio system was still in full force, so rather than signing contracts on a film-by-film basis, actors and actresses signed long-term contracts with individual studios and remained under the authority of the studio head during that period. These men not only dictated which film roles one could accept, but many aspects of an actor's personal life as well. A legion of talent scouts remained occupied with finding and developing young talent, so not even the star of the studio could rest easy or make outlandish demands for fear of being eventually replaced. For an actor to pursue a separate project, he was required to be "loaned out" by his studio in either an artist exchange or some financially advantageous arrangement.

Some actors were recruited based on their appearance alone, signing contracts before taking screen tests or ever having been on a stage or set. Others became overnight sensations, darlings of the public for decades. Only a few of these turned out to be excellent actors, but one of them was certainly Tyrone Power, one of Hollywood's leading men from the 1930s into the 1950s. With a career spanning over 50 films, Power did not have to work through the system, rising to the top almost immediately at the age of 22.

Power was named "King of the Movies" for three straight years (1939 -1941) by fans, and while critics claimed that his success came from his good looks, today he is acknowledged as a good actor, among the most underestimated of this era. Power starred in a variety of film genres, and at least some contemporaries made note of his "remarkable acting range."[1] This included several musicals such as *Alexander's Ragtime Band*, *Second Fiddle*, *Rose of Washington Square*, and *The Eddy Duchin Story*. He also made appearances in several dramas, including *Johnny Apollo*, *Witness for the Prosecution*, *Crash Drive*, and *The Razor's Edge*. Power was even known for a good comedic sense in films like *The Luck of the Irish*, *That Wonderful Urge*, and *Love is News*.

---

[1] Tyrone Power, A Brief Biography – www.tyrone-power.com/biography_tv.html

For most viewers, however, Power was the best swashbuckler in the business, the perfect heir to Errol Flynn and the Fairbanks men. *The Mask of Zorro* has been immortalized in Hollywood history alongside *The Black Swan, Prince of Foxes, The Black Rose*, and *Captain from Castile*, and thanks to his "seemingly charmed life,"[2] Power appeared with the best actors and actresses of his era and was directed by some of the biggest names in the business. He "traveled in circles of influential filmmakers, was loved by moviegoers, and was recognized as King of the Fox lot."[3] Within six months of his first breakout role, imprints of his feet and hands were placed in cement at the famous Grauman's Chinese Theatre. The inscription bore a tribute to the theatrical legacy of his family: "To Sid – following in my father's footsteps."[4]

---

[2] Tyrone Power, A Brief Biography

[3] Tyrone Power, A Brief Biography

[4] IMDB, Tyrone Power, Biography – www.imdb.com

Power's Early Years

"I've done an awful lot of stuff that's a monument to public patience." – Tyrone Power

Tyrone Power was born in Cincinnati, Ohio on May 5, 1914, the only son of an English-born stage and screen actor named Frederick Tyrone Edmund Power. The son of concert pianist Harold Littledale Power, Frederick, who generally went by the name of Fred, married Helen Emma "Patia" Reaume, a talented stage and film actress. Thus, Tyrone's ancestry was Irish, English, German, French Huguenot, and French-Canadian.

Power's father

Power was born right around the start of World War I, and his generation experienced much of their youth during the "Great Depression." At the same time, they enjoyed a rapid pace of technological innovations, particularly when it came to the telephone, radio, and the development of cinema.

In this sense, he fit right in, because Power descended from a long line of well-known theater actors, dating back to his great-grandfather, the Irish actor and comedian Tyrone Power (1797-1841). His great-uncle Maurice was a Shakespearian actor who died in 1849, while his grandfather wrote a two-volume collection entitled *Impressions of America: During the Years 1833, 1834, and 1835*. Other distant relations include Laurence Olivier, widely hailed as the greatest Shakespearean actor of the 20th century. They were related through Power's paternal great-grandmother, Anne Gilbert, who was Olivier's grandmother and also a well-known actress. Power was also related through marriage to author Arthur Evelyn Waugh and through a distant relative to Tyrone Guthrie, the founder of the Stratford Festival in eastern Canada.

Olivier and Joan Fontaine in 1940

Frederick Power was acknowledged to be a fine actor, but he was largely absent in his son's life due to his many stage commitments in New York City, as well as having a penchant for adultery. Young Tyrone was a sickly child, and his mother followed a doctor's suggestion that they relocate to

California, a move they made in 1915. Around this time, Tyrone gained a sister, Anne Power, who later became Anne Lavenue Power Hardenbergh. Frederick and his wife "Patia" appeared together on stage in 1917, the year in which their movie *The Planter* was released, but they drifted apart after that and were divorced in 1920.

Patia continued to work as a stage actress with various regional organizations and with stage stock companies, and at the age of seven, Power appeared with her in the mission play *La Golondrina* in a San Gabriel, California production. She eventually returned to Cincinnati to become the drama and vocal coach at Schuster-Martin School of Drama, coaching her son privately at home. He attended the preparatory school of the University of Dayton.

By the age of 16, Power worked as an usher at the Orpheum Theater of Cincinnati and attended Catholic school, including the Xavier Academy from grades 7-9. Encouraged by the career of his father, he took a keen interest in acting, and after graduating from Purcell High School in 1931, where he played the lead in the school play *Officer 666,* he joined his father for a summer in Quebec at the age of 17, mostly as an observer. Frederick was impressed by his son's "persistence."[5] With his father in the cast, he played as a "super" in six performances of *The Merchant of Venice* at the Chicago Civic Auditorium.

On December 31 of that year, the elder Powell was in his rooms at the Athletic Club after a day working on a movie, *The Miracle Man*, when he suffered a massive heart attack and died in his son's arms. Unsettled from the experience, all the young Power's professional considerations were changed in an instant. After his father's funeral in Aux Noix, Quebec, Power began to go from door to door in California to find any work he could as an actor, but there was none to be had. Without his father, he was penniless and in desperate need of experience.

Instant Stardom

"Tyrone Power was Saturday afternoons!" – Piper Laurie

After landing a bit part in the 1932 production of

---

[5] Factinate, Dashing Facts about Tyrone Power, Hollywood's Doomed Leading Man – www.factinate.com/people/facts-tyrone-power/

Tom Brown of Culver, starring movie actor Tom Brown, Power hoped to parlay the appearance into something bigger, but no doors opened for him except an appearance as little more than an extra in *Flirtation Walk*. Finding himself frozen out of the movies, he began seeking out community theater parts. In 1933, he appeared at the Pasadena Community Playhouse in *Low and Behold*, but after that, he signed on as chauffeur for one of his father's friends, screenwriter Arthur Caesar.

Caesar

Caesar advised Power to head for New York City

to bolster his experience as a stage actor, and Power took his advice, but along the way, he stopped in Chicago for a visit with his friend Don Ameche, who convinced him to stay for a while and make some radio appearances. Ameche was a radio personality for the "Little Theatre off Times Square" for NBC Radio. The low point came when Power was asked to read the comic strips over the airwaves. There was no foothold to be had in radio, so he went on to New York, where he soon met his first true advocate.

Katharine Cornell was among the most celebrated stage actresses from the 1920s-1950s, and she cast Power as an understudy for Burgess Meredith in *Flowers of the Forest*. In a better opportunity, she cast him again in the role of Benvolio in *Romeo and Juliet*, and almost immediately, Power was noticed by Hollywood scouts, who offered him a screen test. Cornell advised against it and told Power to wait until he had more experience. Instead, she assured him that the scouts would be back and gave him a role in her next stage play, *St. Joan*.

Cornell and Guthrie McClintic

As it turned out, Cornell was correct. The scouts returned and again offered Power a screen test, and this time, the actress deemed him ready to go on, so he returned to Hollywood and signed with 20th Century Fox. Almost immediately after a nearly anonymous trial run in *Northern Frontier* (1935) and a few slow starts, he became a top leading man for years to come, known throughout the industry as "everyone's romantic lead."[6] In part, he was signed by 20th Century Fox as their answer to MGM's Robert Taylor.

Taylor

Power was first slated to act in the film *Sing Baby Sing* at the request of actress Alice Faye, a major star for the studio, but director Sidney Lanfield saw

---

no potential whatsoever in the young actor and summarily removed him from the cast, telling him to seek another line of work and insisting that he would never become an actor. Undaunted, Faye convinced the studio to give Power another chance, so he was assigned a small part in *Girl's Dormitory*. Despite his brief appearance, he caught the eye of many fans, among them the famous radio gossip Hedda Hopper, who stayed for several showings to find out who the young man was. Faye would later say of Power, "He wasn't arrogant. He wasn't full of himself, but I've never seen anyone as handsome as Ty."

Faye

Girl's Dormitory was sufficient to land Power a somewhat larger role in *Ladies in Love*, which starred Janet Gaynor, Constance Bennett, and Loretta Young. Still, 20th Century Fox had decided not to pick up his option, so Power took charge and went to visit Henry King to ask for a role. He would have settled for nearly any type of appearance, but King, impressed with his looks and poise, offered him the lead in *Lloyd's of London*. King later said of him, "Tyrone Power was one of the genuine professionals among the actors I've dealt with. I suppose 'craftsman' might be another proper term."

Ladies in Love had come out not long before *Lloyd's of London*, and it claimed to have been based on a play by Ladislaus Bus-Fekete originally called *Three Girls*, but no performances referencing that name have ever been found. Regardless, Power's "cinematic dalliance" brought in so much fan mail that he immediately overtook Don Ameche for the principal role. Ameche's hold on the part of Jonathan Blake was tentative, and he was only "penciled in."

Lloyd's of London was the breakout role Power needed, and it turned him into an instant star. Loretta Young was to be the leading lady but walked out when she found her role was being downsized to make room for Power's "star build-up" treatment by the studio, and she was replaced by Madeleine Carroll. Thus began a long personal and professional friendship between Power and King, who noted, "I'm proud of the fact that Ty and I got along so famously, both on screen and off. We were good friends."

King

The film received rave reviews, and in reference to Power, *Variety Magazine* told readers, "He has looks and acting ability. The women ought to go for him in a big way."[7] The *Los Angeles Examiner*

---

[7] Tyrone Power, King of 20th Century Fox – www.tyrone-power.com/lloydsoflondon-story.html

praised him by suggesting, "Not in a long time has there been a player so dynamic and promising."[8] The *New York Herald Tribune* wrote, "The chief acting is done by Tyrone Power."[9]

Power was billed fourth in the credits but enjoyed by far the most screen time, walking in as an unknown and walking out a "superstar."[10] Loosely based on a study of the trillion-dollar insurance company, the script is filled with both insurance fraud and love, as well as a few good "moments of dry humor."[11]

In 1937, Power starred in *Café Metropole,* the story of a young American in debt to a Parisian nightclub owner. He is forced to court a wealthy heiress in hopes of stealing her fortune. In the same year, he appeared in *Ali Baba Goes to Town* as himself. That movie was one of several reworkings of Mark Twain novels, in this case *A Connecticut Yankee in King Arthur's Court*. A hobo stumbles onto a movie set and dreams that he's been caught up in an Arabian Nights adventure.

---

[8] Tyrone Power

[9] Tyrone Power

[10] Tyrone Power, A Brief Biography

[11] Archive.org, Lloyd's of London, by Henry King – www.archive.org/1936LloydsofLondon

Café Metropole featured co-star Loretta Young. Included in the "Tyrone Power Matinee Idol" DVD collection are two scenes of Bill "Bojangles" Robinson dancing that have been restored, along with all of Power's best work.

Young

For his third film of 1937, Power starred in *Thin Ice*, directed by Sidney Lanfield, who had rejected him outright just a year before. Sonja Henie co-starred as a world skating champion in a story about a Swiss hotel's skating and skiing instructor who falls in love with a man who skis at a regular time each morning. In a few of the scenes, Power actually skis in tandem with Henie, who was a virtuoso on skates, and some of the outdoor scenes were shot at Mount Rainier in Washington State. Power stars as a prince sent on a diplomatic mission in which he was to "play dumb."[12]

[12] Variety Magazine.com, Thin Ice – www.variety.com/film/reviews/thin-ice-1200411309/

Henie

Power engaged in a lengthy affair with Henie, and when she was out of town, he wrote to her explaining that the studio had instructed him to escort Janet Gaynor around, a dubious claim. Allegedly, Henie and Power "had sex all the time in her dressing room, and when they would emerge, Tyrone would look as if he was ready to keel over."[13]

By the end of 1937, Power had filmed *Second Honeymoon* with Loretta Young. In the film, a newly married woman bored with her businessman husband runs across her first playboy husband. In one memorable scene, Power lights two cigarettes in his mouth, starting a fad that was duplicated years later by Paul Henreid in *Now, Voyager*.

In 1938, Power rejoined Alice Faye and Don Ameche in the drama *In Old Chicago*. The plot recounts the story of the O'Leary brothers, honest Jack and rogue Dion, who become powerful rivals on the eve before the city's great fire. The film was directed by Henry King, and the 20-minute fire sequence for *In Old Chicago* cost $150,000 and burned for three days on the studio lot. The casting of Alice Faye came at Power's insistence.

Also in 1938, the cast of *In Old Chicago* reunited for *Alexander's Ragtime Band*, with music by Irving Berlin. The film was a showcase of ragtime song and dance that depicts 1915 San Francisco, and in the process of featuring 29 iconic songs by Berlin, it was based on his 1911 tune of the title. Producer

---

Darryl Zanuck wanted to film a realistic biography of Berlin, but the famous musician would have none of it, agreeing only to a loose facsimile. Regardless, it was "a monument to Irving Berlin,"[14] coming at a cost of $2 million for three months of shooting.

Zanuck

In 1938, during the filming of *Jesse James*, Henry

---

[14] Tcm.com, Alexander's Ragtime Band, 1938 – www.tcm.com/tcmb/title/66978

King offered Power the chance to accompany him in his private plane to the location shoot in Missouri. Along the way, Power became fascinated with the instrument panel, and King allowed him to take the controls for a brief period. Upon his return to Hollywood, Power took flying lessons, a hobby that was to become one of his greatest joys through the years. He was soon an accomplished, licensed pilot.

While shooting *Jesse James*, Power had a fling with a local girl who became pregnant. She put the child up for adoption and Power spent a small fortune over the next decade trying without success to find him.

Jesse James employed six filming locations in Missouri, as well as one in Los Angeles and another in Jamestown, California. The bulk of it was filmed in McDonald County, and every citizen "was agog"[15] to see Tyrone Power and Henry Fonda having coffee at the local café or wandering around the set. The demands on the town were many, including buggies, wagons, surreys, dozens of horses, and an antique train. Around 150 extras were hired from

---

[15] Joplin Globe, Bill Caldwell: McDonald County was agog as film crew arrived to shoot Jesse James, July 30, 2016 - www.joplinglobe.comnews/local_news/

town, and crowds that appeared to watch the filming averaged about 5,000 people at a time.

  In 1938, Power was already so popular that he finished "right behind Shirley Temple"[16] in the volume of incoming fan mail. In 1939, he was loaned out to MGM Studios for one production, *Marie Antoinette.* Gary Cooper had been in the running for the male lead, but Norma Shearer pleaded for Power. Zanuck felt that the role was too small and was ill-suited to his personality, vowing never to loan him again.

  Suez was also completed in 1938, and in the film, Power co-starred again with Loretta Young. Unlucky in love, Ferdinand de Lesseps is sent as a junior diplomat to the Isthmus of Suez and realizes that it is the ideal spot for a canal. Zanuck had a major row with the censors over the character played by young Annabella wearing a revealing wet shirt, and the real De Lesseps' family sued the studio because Power's character had a romance with Annabella. They eventually discarded the case, deciding that the offending scene was not

[16] Classic Hollywood #115, Stuff Nobody Cares About, Tyrone Power "No good Reason to get married" –
www.stuffnobodycaresabout.com/2021/07/25/classic-hollywood-115-tyrone-power/

detrimental to the honor of France after all.

In a newspaper article that year, Lucie Neville asked a group of male stars why they did not want to get married. Nearly everyone gave a financial answer, which was somewhat understandable since alimony was at the time a one-sided arrangement. However, when Neville got to Power, he thought for a moment before saying, "I just don't want to get married. Now, I've often wished I had a good answer to that question, 'Why haven't you married?' but I can't name one except I just don't want to."[17]

The following April, he married the French actress known as Annabella. At that time, Power was among the leading bachelors in Hollywood, and Annabella (born Suzanne Georgette Charpentier) was among the most sought-after stage and screen stars in Europe, with high popularity in the U.S. as well. Born near Paris, she was the daughter of a publisher.

[17] Classic Hollywood #115

Power and Annabella

They met at 20th Century Fox, as Annabella appeared in numerous movies on both sides of the Atlantic. When Zanuck realized that the romance was serious, he strongly objected, fearing that Power would lose much of his female base, so he offered Anabella plum roles in European projects to get her out of the country, but the persistent actress went against his wishes. Her career suffered greatly as Zanuck refused to assign her to any roles, so she resorted to a return to stage acting.

Zanuck basically suspended her from the studio, but Annabella still had a husband waiting in France and was not in a hurry to repatriate. Power and Annabella appeared together in several radio broadcasts, including *Blood and Sand*, *The Rage of Manhattan*, and *Seventh Heaven*. The first was an adaptation of the film Power would later appear in with Rita Hayworth, while the other two were designed for Lux Radio, a program that featured the largest drama anthology collection in the world of radio.

Power and Annabella also appeared in the stage play *Liliom* at the Country Playhouse in Westport, Connecticut. *Liliom*, a steamy and dysfunctional love story, was first presented in 1909 in Budapest, resulting in a theatrical failure. However, in New York, it was a "rare event."[18] The play by Ferenc

---

[18] New York Times

Molnar went on to become *Carousel* by Rodgers & Hammerstein. In that period, Power worked with Humphrey Bogart, Jeanne Crain, Loretta Young, Alice Faye, and Al Jolson.

Somewhat incredibly, when the young star tried to buy a house, he was stunned to discover that he was nearly broke. Upon investigation, it turned out he had been swindled by his business manager, his uncle Frank, who stole much of his income. However, Power was never one for confrontation - instead of making a scene, he did his best to "keep the scandal on the down-low."[19]

Annabella and Power persisted and were eventually married in 1939. Power adopted her daughter Annie. Annabella had every intention of giving up her performing career, but she became increasingly obsessed with the war news at home in Europe. Volunteering for the Red Cross, she also returned to the stage and her home life began to crumble.

In 1939, *Second Fiddle* was released, a story in which a studio publicist takes a Minnesota skating

---

[19] Factinate

teacher to Hollywood, but when she returns home, he follows her. Sonja Henie again starred with Power. The search for the female lead was so exhaustive, much like the eternal search for Scarlett in *Gone with the Wind*, that the script became riddled with *Gone with the Wind* jokes. The world premiere was held at the Roxy Theater in New York.

In *Day-Time Wife*, also released in 1939, Power co-starred with Linda Darnell in the story of a young wife who discovers that her new husband is involved with his beautiful secretary. She applies for a secretarial job with his business rival. Darnell played Power's wife at the age of just 16.

The Rose of Washington Square opened in the same year with Power, Alice Faye, and Al Jolson. It is a story in which a singer joins the Ziegfeld Follies, but her marriage to a con man poses problems for her career. It resembles the life of entertainer Fanny Brice, and Power's role is similar to the character of Nicky Arnstein in the later production of *Funny Girl*.

Hollywood Hobbies, in which Power played

himself, as he would in several cameo appearances, was a brief lead-up to his first drama of 1939, entitled *The Rains Came*, co-starring Myrna Loy. In India, a married British aristocrat is reunited with an old flame, but she has her sights set on a handsome surgeon.

Recreating the floods of *The Rains Came* required 33 million gallons of water, and out of the 100 days it took to shoot, half were spent in man-made rains and floods. Power became the first performer to win the Harvard Lampoon's Worst Actor Award for *The Rains Came*. Zanuck joked that he was relieved it was not for *Marie Antoinette*.

Brigham Young, the story of the Mormons' powerful leader, was filmed with Power in the lead and traces the story of the Mormon congregation following Young to a new "promised land" in Utah.

The Swashbuckler

"I'm sick of all these knights in shining armor parts, I want to do something worthwhile like plays and films that have something to say." – Tyrone Power

Power switched his screen persona for a time with *Johnny Apollo*, in which the son of a jailed Wall Street broker turns to crime to pay for his father's release. In the scene where father and son converse, a photo of Power's real mother can be seen in the background. Linda Darnell was to have played the original role, and Alice Faye was also considered until Zanuck was able to borrow Dorothy Lamour from Paramount in exchange for Don Ameche for another film.

The first of Power's great swashbuckler films was released in 1940, and it remains his most famous: *The Mark of Zorro*, co-starring Linda Darnell. One of several versions, a young Spanish aristocrat must masquerade as a fop to maintain his secret identity of Zorro as he restores justice to California.

A promotional poster for the movie

The Mark of Zorro was a remake of the original 1920 version starring Douglas Fairbanks. Many viewers did not believe that Power could match Fairbank's acrobatic abilities, and he never really tried. However, the duel with Basil Rathbone has gone down as one of the finest filmed swordfights of all time. In fact, "Power's swordplay was more praised than his wordplay."[20] *The Mark of Zorro* was a tale that originated in the legend of *The Curse of Capistrano*. Basil Rathbone, himself an expert theatrical swordsman, was quoted as saying, "Power was the most agile man with a sword I've ever faced before a camera."[21]

A lobby card for the movie

---

[20] IMDB

[21] IMDB

The Mark of Zorro was filmed in a number of Mexican locations in black and white. It was nominated for Best Original Music Score and named to the National Film Registry by the Library of Congress. A horde of television and film sequels ensued over the next two decades. One review for Rotten Tomatoes hailed Power as "excellent as both fop and fox."[22]

In 1941, Power appeared in *Three of a Kind* as himself with Jack Benny and Randolph Scott. Co-starring with Rita Hayworth in the drama *Blood and Sand* in the same year, Power played the part of an illiterate peasant who rises to fame as a matador. His fame is complicated by an affair with a beautiful aristocrat.

The remake of a 1922 melodrama with Rudolph Valentino, *Blood and Sand* was filmed in the Plaza de Toros of Mexico City. Despite being a bullfighting film, it was a natural follow-up to *The Mark of Zorro*, and it "capitalized on the lucrative romantic pairing…of Power and Linda Darnell,"[23] a rare occasion in which Rita Hayworth was not in the

---

[22] IMDB

[23] Four Star Films, Blood and Sand (1941) – www.fourstarfilms.com2019/03.17/blood-and-sand-1941/

romantic forefront. Vincente Blasco Ibanez's novel of the same name is a "Spanish national epic"[24] that tells of the rise and fall of Juan Gallardo, the famous matador. The film bears definitive proof of Power's acting range, as he "shows he can handle serious dramatic roles."[25]

One of several war films in which Power appeared was *A Yank in the RAF* in 1941. It starred Betty Grable, and Power plays an American pilot who joins the Royal Air Force just to impress his girlfriend.

A year later, Power filmed *This Above All*, co-starring with Joan Fontaine. In this film, aristocrat Prudence Cathaway defies convention by joining the WAAFS and becomes romantically involved with an AWOL soldier. In real life, Power's flying stunt double was shot down by German aircraft, and he was taken prisoner one year later. Similarly, one of the camera operators and an aerial photographer were shot down over England. The film was based on real-life experiences of American volunteers in the RAF, and Power reprised the role soon after for

[24] tmc.com

[25] tmc.com

an edition of Lux Radio Theater.

In 1942, Power filmed *The Black Swan* with Maureen O'Hara. Another swashbuckler, this pirate movie featured an ex-pirate who contends with rowdy buccaneers and a love-hate relationship with an aristocratic woman who's tougher than she seems. *The Black Swan* was filmed in Jamaica, Honduras, Cuba, and Mexico, with a few additional American locations. Though never really impressed with his general film output, Power "must have been pleased with *The Black Swan*."[26]

---

[26] tmc.com

A picture of the trailer for *The Black Swan*

Son of Fury: The Story of Benjamin Blake was released in 1942 as well, and it has been described as a "98-minute epic tale of redemption."[27] Blake, a bonded servant, is accused of escaping and attempting to murder his sister in the time of King George before his real identity as a nobleman is finally revealed.

Son of Fury was the film that starred Power and

[27] Cliff Aliperti, Tyrone Power in Son of Fury: The Story of Benjamin Blake (1942), Immortal Ephemera – www.immortalephemera.com

Gene Tierney for the first time, and they would meet again in *The Razor's Edge* and *That Wonderful Urge*. Power played Blake's father in a prologue explaining how he and his wife had been done away with by the uncle, but it was cut from the film to add suspense.

Tierney and Power in *The Razor's Edge*

Crash Dive was Power's last movie before joining World War II. The story involves a submarine lieutenant and his commander who fall in love with the same woman. A "crash dive" is a high-speed evasive maneuver that involves blowing the air tanks and engaging the propeller to dive at a steep angle. It is still used to avoid impending midair collisions. The film co-starred Anne Baxter, and Power was allowed to defer his arrival date until the movie was finished shooting. Fittingly, his credit in the film reads, "Tyrone Power, U.S.M.C.R."

In the wake of Pearl Harbor, Power enlisted in the Marine Corps. With no collegiate background, he did not qualify for Officer Candidate School at Quantico, and he refused his studio's efforts to help him get around that requirement. Power's goal had been to become a glider pilot, and he delayed entry to finish filming *Crash Dive* before boot camp in San Diego. By the time he reached the rank of Lieutenant, he had 180 solo hours.

Due to his previous flight experience, Power was assigned to an accelerated flight program at the NCAS in Corpus Christi, Texas as a multi-engine pilot, and he earned his wings in 1944. He then attended Flight Instrument School at NAS Atlanta, standard procedure for transport pilots.

An established star already, Power was "prepared to put his career on hold."[28] In a Newsletter of

Marine Air Transport, Jerry Taylor, a retired USMC flight instructor, recalled, "He was an excellent student, never forgot a procedure I showed him or anything I told him."[29] He was somewhat of a danger lover, but "thrived as a pilot."[30]

As a Lieutenant, he served in the Pacific Theater, reassigned from El Centro to Kwajalein in the Marshall Islands and flying out of Saipan in the Marianne Islands for the VMR – 352 squadron. He carried supplies aboard a R5C (Curtis-46 Commando derived from commercial high-altitude airliner design) into Iwo Jima, and he was also tasked with airlifting wounded Americans, often under heavy fire. Navigator Jim Powell explained, "He was a quiet guy who kept to himself, but he treated the rest of us well."[31] Powell noted one mission in which Power was instructed to ditch the plane in the water: "He flew in at 50 feet above the water [with] the island under heavy assault, [and] low on fuel. There was a pea soup fog, but the ocean was like glass. Power made a perfect landing.

---

[28] Tyrone-power.com

[29] Tyrone-power.com

[30] Factinate

[31] Tyrone-power.com

Within 15 minutes, the plane sank [and] the Coast Guard picked us up. Power broke his leg getting out of the plane."[32]

Power came home with the American Campaign Medal, the Asiatic Campaign Medal, two bronze stars and the World War II Victory Medal. Promoted to Captain, he remained in the reserves and was not recalled to Korea.

Marital troubles with Annabella awaited Power at home, but they committed themselves to working it out. Upon his discharge to Seattle, they went on a second honeymoon to recover from the wartime experiences. Both cheated on the other, Annabella with Roald Dahl and Power with Judy Garland, who tried desperately to convince him to leave his wife.

Power appeared as himself in the 1943 *Show Business at War*, and the first role Power played after the war was in *The Razor's Edge*, a wartime drama. Based on a philosophical novel by W. Somerset Maugham published in 1944, it is based on the dichotomy of materialism versus spirituality. Set in Chicago, Paris, and India in the 1920s and

---

[32] Tyrone-power.com

1930s, Power took the role of Larry Darrell, a World War I aviator who returns home rejecting his pre-war values and seeking "the meaning of human existence."[33]

The Razor's Edge is among the first novels to propose non-Western solutions to society's ills, and reviews of the film were favorable. The *New York Times* wrote, "A hardened Tyrone Power was surprisingly convincing."[34] The film was nominated for Best Picture at the Academy Awards. Barry Bradford, a critic, author, motivational speaker, and historian, claimed that Power was too old for the role, though not necessarily because of his age: "Only 30, he looks 35 and acts more mature than that."[35] In part, he faulted the director and lighting designer for the problem.

Power fought hard to land his next role in the film noir *Nightmare Alley*, over the objections of Zanuck, who believed it would hurt his image. Although he received excellent reviews, he felt betrayed by Zanuck, who pulled the release and

[33] Britannica, The 1940s – www.britannica.com/biography/Edmund-Goulding#ref1177586

[34] Britannica

[35] Barry Bradford, The Razor's Edge – A Frustrating and Fascinating Film – www.barrybradford.com/razors-edge-frustrating-fascinating-film/

most of its promotion. In effect, the producer simply "took it out of circulation."[36]

Based on the 1946 novel by William Lindsay Gresham, the plot follows a carnival worker "eager for higher stakes."[37] He runs off with a co-worker to start a mentalist game directed at Chicago high society. It is a "dark and cynical film,"[38] neither a mystery nor a thriller. Rather, it "induces a soul-sickness feeling."[39] *Nightmare Alley* propagates the enduring suggestion that "we're all susceptible to being taken in."[40] The preface to the *New York Times* review of *Nightmare Alley* commented both on Power's uncharacteristic portrayal and the problem of getting the film before the public at all: "With Tyrone Power in the lead, the first adaptation had to find ways to tell the story of a soul sickness that wouldn't offend censors."[41]

A full 10-acre carnival was built on the back lot of Fox, and over 100 sideshow attractions were added. It was Power himself who had requested purchasing

---

[36] IMDB

[37] NY Times, The 1947 'Nightmare Alley': A Dark View of Class as Destiny – www.nytimes.com2021/12/19/nightmare-alley-1947.html

[38] NY Times

[39] NY Times

[40] NY Times

[41] NY Times

the rights to the novel. *Nightmare Alley* remains what is widely regarded as Power's best performance. "It is a dark role he insisted on playing; his transformation in the last section of the film is so startling that it is believable when he's not recognized by his friends."[42] In the limited circulation the film still enjoyed, Zanuck ordered a reunion scene to be "tacked on"[43] to avoid ending the film on such a downbeat note.

---

[42] Laura Grieve

[43] IMDB

A 1946 portrait of Power

1947 found Power back to normal acting fare in *Captain from Castile*. Filmed in Mexico, the gossip grapevine sizzled when Lana Turner visited him there on the set, presumably to celebrate Annabella's announcement of their separation, citing "incompatibility of careers." That was good news for Zanuck, who wanted *Nightmare Alley* and Annabella to both disappear. So appalled was he at seeing Power in *Nightmare Alley* that he accelerated the release date of *Captain from Castile* to take the taste of it out of the public's mouths. The rehearsal and shooting process were generally rushed.

Lana Turner's love life had always been complicated. Beside her many lovers, she had married seven times (or eight if counting the fact she married Stephen Crane twice), but she claimed Power was the love of her life. They had been acquaintances for many years, but he was married to Annabella. After his separation, he invited Lana to his house for a cocktail, kissed her, and she was "hooked forever."[44]

---

[44] Lana Turner.com, Lanta Turner and Tyrone Power – www.lana-turner.com/lana-turner-and-tyrone-power/

Turner

During the Mexico visit, she was supposed to be filming *Green Dolphin Street* and was not allowed to leave the shooting location. She thought that they would marry soon and had become pregnant. She was surprisingly "thrilled about that,"[45] at least in the beginning, but she soon became aware that the

---

[45] Lana Turner.com

pregnancy would mean "career death."

The *Captain from Castile* was filmed in Michoacán for the most part, and during this time, the volcano Paricutin erupted, causing all kinds of problems. The lighting was difficult to set, and the film grew more expensive by the day. Jonathan Yardley of *The Washington Post* wrote that the film had "enough swashbuckling action to keep the Three Musketeers busy for years."[46]

As a planned "barnstorming" trip drew nearer, covering 32,000 miles and visiting 18 countries, life seemed be fun again for a while. Power received an honorary degree in Arts from the University of Tampa and delivered the 1948 commencement speech. He kept a copy of every script of his career, and some he was interested in playing. They were all bound, and he enjoyed looking over them.

That Wonderful Urge was released in 1948, co-starring Gene Tierney. When an heiress realizes that the friendly young man she just met is really an investigative reporter, she ruins his career by claiming that they are married. Power had starred in

[46] Legacy, The Swashbuckling Tyrone Power – www.legacy.com/news/celebrity-deaths/the-swashbuckling-tyrone-power/

the original version of *Love is News* nine years earlier with Loretta Young.

Luck of the Irish was released in the same year. The story involves a grateful leprechaun who follows an American reporter from Ireland to New York, serving as the newsman's conscience and servant. Based on a novel entitled *There Was a Little Man* by Guy Pearce Jones and Constance Bridges Jones, Power co-starred with Anne Baxter.

Power was not thrilled at all by Turner's pregnancy, finding it coarse and unseemly to be married (even if separated) while having a child with another woman, so he was relieved to depart on what was supposed to be a 12-week trip around the world by air. The night before he left, Turner threw a $10,000 "Bon Voyage" party for him against his wishes at Ciro's, a famous nightclub in Hollywood.

During their affair, Turner was constantly on the lookout for rivals. She allegedly pressed a pot of hot coffee into the bare arm of French actress Corrine Calvet before apologizing for the "accident." She had no way of knowing that Calvet was not the true threat - that came from an up-and-comer named

Linda Christian, a bit player in *Green Dolphin
Street* and the next Mrs. Power.

Christian

On September 17, 1948, while Power was on his
city-hopping adventure, Turner used their
prearranged code to tell him that she decided to have
an abortion. If the answer was "yes," she was to say,
"I found the house today."[47] Giving up the child of

her greatest love is said to have been "the hardest thing Lana ever did in her life."[48]

Reportedly, Howard Strickling, "the MGM fixer,"[49] made all the arrangements for the abortion. He was rumored to have done the same thing for Power and Judy Garland when she allegedly became pregnant after their affair in the early 1940s.

Everyone assumed that Turner and Power would marry and were surprised when he took off in a plane dubbed "The Geek,"[50] furnished by Howard Hughes, for a journey around much of the world. Bob Buck served as co-pilot after being hired by his boss, Hughes, to take care of the plane. The flight engineer was Bill Agner, with Bob Stevens as navigator and Bill Ritter as radio operator. Jim Denton, a 20th Century Fox public relations man, went along for the ride, and Bill Gallagher, Power's secretary, rounded out the crew. Buck understood the reason for the timing, which was to get away from Lana Turner. He empathized, observing, "No man had the right to be that handsome."[51]

---

[47] Lana Turner.com

[48] Lana Turner.com

[49] Amo Mama

[50] Tyrone Power, a Brief Biography

Power's journey, spent for the most part behind the controls of the plane, included Puerto Rico, Liberia, Southwest Africa, Italy, British Guyana, Gold Coast, South Africa, Ethiopia, Brazil, the Belgian Congo, Portugal, Sudan, Ireland, Goose Bay, Labrador, Canada, Kenya, Greenland, England, France, and Greece.

"The Geek," named for Power's role in *Nightmare Alley,* was a big silver DC3. Crossing four continents, Power seemed "rested and refreshed"[52] on his return, even though he had done 90% of the flying. On the nose of the plane were painted 18 flags. Along the way, he had an audience with the pope, Emperor Haile Selassie of Ethiopia, and Field Marshall Smuts of South Africa.

In response to his first question upon returning, he said that "the prettiest girls collectively…were in Iceland."[53] He had planned to be gone for six weeks, but the trip took three months. Among his highlights was hearing a girl in Dallas telling a reporter that she would faint if Tyrone Power came up to say

---

[51] Lady Eve's Reel Life, Remembering Tyrone Power, Aug. 25, 2012 – www.ladyevesreallife.com/2012/08

[52] Tyrone-power.com

[53] Tyrone-power.com

hello. He got out of his cab and did just that. The
girl did not faint but emitted a "ladylike scream"[54]
that pleased him to no end. Dangers that put a thrill
in the flight for Power included gas tank leaks
leaving Brazil, a bad weather landing in Monrovia,
and subzero weather between Ireland and Iceland.
Once he returned to America, he spent his time
redecorating his home and working on *That Old
Magic* for the studio.

An Abrupt End

"Some day I will show all the [people] who say I
was a success just because of my pretty face.
Sometimes I wish I had a really bad car accident so
my face would get smashed up and I'd look like
Eddie Constantine." – Tyrone Power

During his visit to Rome, Power met the beautiful
starlet Linda Christian, who must have gotten her
hands on Power's itinerary and planned their
meeting. Christian was an international actress when
she became Power's second wife. Born with the
name Blanca Rosa Welter in Tampico, Mexico to a
Dutch oil executive, she was half Dutch and half

---

[54] Tyrone-power.com

Mexican. Christian was discovered by Errol Flynn in Acapulco, and she went on to become the first "Bond girl"[55] and a favorite model for painter Diego Rivera. She spent her youth in Venezuela, the Middle East, Holland, and South Africa.

Power had serious doubts about Lana Turner, whom he suspected of carrying on another romance with Frank Sinatra, so he married Christian in January 1949 at Rome's Church of Santa Francesca, with an estimated 10,000 screaming fans in attendance. Christian arrived late, and marrying Tyrone Power was her chief claim to fame. Following their wedding next to the Roman Colosseum, they were welcomed by Pope Pius XII. It was dubbed the "wedding of the century."

Christian's intelligence was at times underestimated since she could be very quiet at parties, but she was highly educated and fluent in half a dozen languages, a superb dancer and championship-level swimmer. One contemporary explained, "When it comes to fun, she can be as noisy as the moment suggests."[56]

____

[55] Altfg.com, Linda Christian: First Bond Girl, Tyrone Power Wife and Diego Rivera Model
[56] Tyrone Power, King of 20th Century Fox

Early on, Power had expressed romantic interest in many older women, subjecting himself to "what can best be described as the 'Junior treatment.'"[57] By the time he blossomed professionally, however, that persona was left behind.

Lana Turner assumed that following Power's trip, they would pick up the relationship where they had left off, but that was not to happen. Her feelings for him clearly "far outweighed his"[58] for her. At first, she heard nothing from him before discovering that he had met another woman in Europe. Devastated, she later claimed, "No man except possibly Tyrone Power took the time to find out that I was a human being, not just a pretty, shapely little thing. That could have been my fault. I didn't know myself."[59] Myrna Loy also remembered Power with great fondness, once remarking that he was "one of the nicest human beings she'd ever known – I'm sorry to report that we weren't lovers. I loved him, but he was married to that damn French woman."[60]

Children were to become an uphill battle with

---

[57] Tyrone Power, King of 20th Century Fox

[58] Altfg.com

[59] Lana Turner.com

[60] Lady Eve's Reel Life

Christian. According to interviewer Maria Ciaccia, "They had a very passionate love and a very volatile relationship. She was pregnant almost the entire time they were married and miscarried several times. One child, a son, was stillborn."[61]

In 1950, *The Black Rose* came out, in which a disinherited Saxon nobleman leaves Norman England in the 13th century with an archer friend to seek their fortune in the east. Power was cast with Orson Welles and Cecile Aubrey. It seems a strange role for Welles to accept, but he was forced to earn money to continue funding his project, a film adaptation of *Othello*. Extras were hired from the local brothel, and it was filmed at Warwickshire Castle and several locations in Morocco, including Casablanca.

Also in 1950, Power began rehearsals for *Mr. Roberts*, a stage version in which he performed the title role to sellout crowds for six months in the London Coliseum. The *New York Times* Review led off by telling readers, "Tyrone Power in Lead, and Jackie Cooper Win Plaudits…Massive Impressive

---

[61] Altfg.com

Set."[62] *Variety Magazine* called it "a magnificent production"[63] and went on to say that "Tyrone Power gives a warm, colorful and meaningful interpretation of the frustrated officer who fears that the war will pass him by before he gets into active service – a major personal success."[64] Power turned a growing rift with Zanuck and 20th Century Fox into an asset with this stage performance.

Power grew disappointed with his most recent assignments as well, including *American Guerilla in the Philippines* (1950), a story of American soldiers stranded in the Philippines after the Japanese invasion who form guerilla bands to fight back. *American Guerilla in the Philippines* was filmed just prior to the outbreak of the Korean War, and the Japanese warships portrayed were refurbished American vessels. Director Fritz Lang made the film to pay the bills, and he later denied having made it at all.

The following year, Power completed *I'll Never Forget You* with co-star Ann Blyth. In the story, a

<hr>

[62] Tyrone-power.com

[63] Tyrone-power.com

[64] Tyrone-power.com

scientist obsessed with the past transports himself back in time to 18th century London and falls in love with a beautiful young woman.

Rawhide (1951) tells the tale of a stagecoach employee and a traveling woman at the mercy of four outlaws. Co-starring with Susan Hayward, it is a well-done "spare outpost Western."[65] As one reviewer put it, Power is "slightly past his prime, but he can still pretty nearly fake it."[66] Power's role was originally intended for Gregory Peck, but it went on to become part of the "Tyrone Power, Matinee Idol" collection.

Pony Soldier, filmed in 1952, followed the story of a Canadian Mounted Policeman who must obtain the release of white hostages from the Cree tribes that continuously raid Montanans from their reservation.

Also that year, Power also finished *Diplomatic Courier*, in which a State Department courier finds himself fighting Soviet agents and seductive women in post-war Europe. Shortly after, Power portrayed

---

[65] Four Star Films

[66] Four Star Films

Senator Dean Edwards on the syndicated radio show *Freedom U.S.A.* He was originally slated to star in *Way of a Gaucho* with Henry King directing, but King requested a transfer to another film, and Power's name disappeared as well.

Power and Christian were able to have two baby girls, Romina Francesca Power and Taryn Power, in 1953, but Power continued to have affairs on the side, most notably with Anita Ekberg on the set of *Mississippi Gambler*. There were others, including Mary Roblee, editor for *Vogue Magazine*. He proposed to her, but it went nowhere. He was at the time also involved with British actress Thelma Faye.

Ekberg

Power and Christian were intended to play the leading roles in *Mississippi Gambler*, but Piper Laurie burst onto the scene with an unforgettable screen test and took it away. Laurie later recalled that she had to "walk on burning coals to get the part."[67] Power filmed *Mississippi Gambler* for Universal Studios and made $1 million for the

[67] Altfg.com

effort, a sizeable sum in that era.

Being unfaithful no longer seemed to bother Power, and he asked his wife, "Why do you worry? Why don't you get yourself a lover, too?"[68] Christian did just that with Edmund Purdom, but despite Power's cavalier attitude, it poisoned the marriage from his perspective. Christian was humiliated by losing the *Mississippi Gambler* role and claimed that her husband should have stood up for her. It spelled the end of their marriage. In addition to the affair with Ekberg, Linda "never forgave her husband"[69] for allowing the role to fall to Piper Laurie. When Power was divorced, the decree allowed Power two months of custody annually with his two daughters, and if his schedule permitted, a longer period.

---

[68] Factinate
[69] IMDB

Laurie

In 1953, Power made *King of the Khyber Rifles*, with Henry King directing. In this film, a half-caste British officer battles the prejudices of his army colleagues and the local population by helping to put down a rebellion begun by a local warlord. Power was considered too old for the role and generally unconvincing as a British officer.

Fox made every attempt to entice Power to return to the studio, offering him a plum role in *The Robe*, but he still turned it down. Instead, he began a run of the play *John Brown's Body* in a four-year-long tour with Judith Anderson and Raymond Massey. *John Brown's Body* provided a demanding role for an experienced stage actor, but Power took it up and excelled. The tour took him 30,000 miles by bus from the opening at Santa Barbara through 40 states and several Canadian provinces. Charles Laughton directed in two tours of 80 performances each. In the middle, the production played on Broadway for eight weeks.

Power in *John Brown's Body*

In 1955, Power was a member of the original
Broadway cast of *The Dark is Light Enough*, a
strange play involving a Hungarian rebellion against
the Austrians and concentrated on the reactions of
the lady of the house. That same year, he appeared
in *The Long Gray Line*, a John Ford film released by
Columbia. Co-starring Maureen O'Hara, the story
involves an Irish immigrant hired at West Point as a

civilian employee who rises to the rank of NCO and Instructor over a 50-year career. A *Spectator Magazine* reviewer referred to the film as "the longest and grayest film"[70] she had ever seen.

As it turned out, *Untamed* was the last picture Power ever made for Fox. He remembered it with a grain of salt, "Fox did a lot for me…[and the] feeling is mutual. Let's face it, though, I've done an awful lot of stuff that's a monument to public patience."[71] In this 19th century story, the character of Katie O'Neill is forced to relocate to South Africa owing to the potato famine in Ireland and runs into an old flame. *Untamed* was set before the Boer Wars (1899-1902), and the film was banned in India for presenting "disparaging" impressions of life in Africa. Many studios rejected the project as too expensive because about 2,500 Zulus were employed as extras. By this time, Power had been working for Fox studios for 18 years.

In 1956, Power was acting in *The Devil's Disciple*, a play authored by George Bernard Shaw. Primarily touring through England, the play made a special

---

[70] IMDB
[71] IMDB

trip to Glasgow, Scotland, where the year before Power had delivered a gift of polio equipment to the local hospital. The welcome to his arrival was understandably effusive.

Christian divorced Power in 1956, and at one point, she was called to testify in an L.A. Court for refusing to return a collection of jewels given her by Robert H. Schlesinger, whose $100,000 check for partial payment bounced. From there, her career faded.

In 1957, *The Story of Eddy Duchin* was filmed, featuring the true story of the famous pianist and band leader. Power's co-star was Kim Novak, with whom he interacted very poorly. Both Joan Fontaine and Eva Marie Saint had read for the part, but despite the lack of chemistry, *The Story of Eddy Duchin* became the 12th highest grossing film of 1956. Of note in the film is that Power pantomimed playing the piano himself, no easy feat.

By this time, Power was working to form a theater company of his own, and he hired author Nora Sayre to read plays for him. She wrote of this time in her book, *On the Wing*, detailing his relationships

with Mai Zetterling and Debbie Minardos.
Zetterling, a Swedish actress, lived with Power from
1956-1958.

Zetterling

Power's old boss, Zanuck, gave him the lead in
The Sun Also Rises in 1957. Co-starring Ava
Gardner with a major appearance by Errol Flynn,
the story follows a group of disillusioned American

expatriate writers in 1920s France and Spain. It was based on Ernest Hemingway's novel of that name published in 1926 and is titled *Fiesta* in England.

While watching the film version of *The Sun Also Rises*, Hemingway walked out after around 25 minutes, claiming that the only good thing about the film was Errol Flynn's part. In the movie, Errol Flynn did not enter until the 53rd minute.

The staff, Hemingway, Power, and Gardner all tried to have Robert Evans fired from the cast. Zanuck said flatly, "The kid stays in the picture."[72] This statement led to a long producing career for Evans.

It was Hemingway who had insisted on the casting of Ava Gardner. Constance Bennett had tried getting the project started 20 years earlier, but it went against the Production Code Administration's rules to mention impotency in a man, and they had to wait for the objecting agent to retire in 1954. Another interesting sidelight was the presence of Pancho Villa's son as Errol Flynn's stand-in.

---

[72] IMDB

At first, Power turned down the role of accused murderer Leonard Vole in *Witness for the Prosecution* of Agatha Christie, to be released in 1957. He told Director Billy Wilder that he simply didn't want to make any more movies. Wilder in turn offered him $300,000 and a percentage of the film, convincing Power to take the role. Also starring Marlene Dietrich and Charles Laughton, the story follows a veteran British barrister who must defend his client in a murder trial that delivers surprise after surprise.

Witness for the Prosecution was one of only two movie versions of Agatha Christie's works that she ever approved of, with the other one being *Murder on the Orient Express*. Principal players were unaware of the ending until the final day of shooting. Billy Wilder was described by one cast member as "two people – Mr. Hyde and Mr. Hyde."[73]

---

[73] IMDB

Power in *Witness for the Prosecution*

Power was also offered $300,000 for two films in that year. In *Witness for the Prosecution*, he was considered by some to be too old, and he was drinking and smoking heavily during that period. Others believed that the role should have gone to someone with a British accent. Nonetheless, after completion of the film, Power declared that it had been one of only three occasions in which he was truly proud of his work. Marlene Dietrich's role of the love-enslaved woman was enhanced by a "real-life crush"[74] on Power. He is said to have been embarrassed by her advances.

---

[74] IMDB

Also in 1957, Power narrated three stories of old Irish country life in *Rising of the Moon* in 1957. Based on a series of short stories, the first was *Majesty of the Law*, in which a police officer must arrest an old-fashioned traditional fellow for assault. His principles evoke much empathy from the whole town. The second is entitled *One Minute's Wait* and is a glimpse into the lives of train passengers who wait at a little country train depot. The third is simply entitled '*1921*,' and is a story about a condemned Irish nationalist and his daring escape. Power introduced each story.

In *Seven Days from Now*, filmed in 1957, also titled *Seven Waves Away* and *Abandon Ship*, Power starred with Zetterling. A ship's officer commands a lifeboat full of survivors of a sunken luxury liner. The "ship survivor" genre was a favorite premise of Hollywood since the Second World War, and its original title was *Seven Waves from Now*.

Seven Days from Now was based on a real event in which the ocean liner *William Brown* is supposed to have struck an iceberg. The American ship sank, with a lifeboat taking 31 passengers. A group of 16 were forced out, and survivors were picked up by the *Crescent*. It was to be the first film of Power's new production company, Copa Productions, Ltd. The decision of who to cast overboard formed the basis of the film's central question, answered by Power with English philosopher Jeremy Bentham's maxim: "the greatest good for the greatest number."[75]

On March 26, 1958, Power appeared in George Bernard Shaw's *Back to Methuselah* at the Ambassador Theater of New York, co-starring Faye Emerson. *Back to Methuselah* is part of a series with a preface entitled *The Infidel Half Century (A Metabiological Pentateuch)*. They include *In the Beginning (Garden of Eden), The Gospel of the Barnabas Brothers (present day), The Thing Happens: A.D. 2170, Tragedy of an Elderly Gentleman, A.D. 3000*, and *As Far as Thought Can Reach, A.D. 31,290*. The play ran for 29 performances at the Ambassador.

In May of that year, Power married Deborah Ann Montgomery Minardos, despite vowing to never marry again. He met Minardos during the run of

---

[75] IMDB

Back to Methuselah, and she was a friend of Linda Christian's brother-in-law. "A bohemian spirit,"[76] she had courted, among others, Elvis Presley. The 26-year-old Minardos was the only American among Power's three wives. They were married in Elvis's hometown of Tunica, Mississippi, and they soon announced that they were expecting their first child. Power as always hoped for a boy to continue his family legacy.

To all who knew him, Power seemed unusually happy during their six-month marriage. He felt confident that "Minardos had no ambitions other than to be his wife, and to have his children, according to Power."[77] She observed, "He's beautiful. Every way there is, he's beautiful."[78]

On September 5, 1958, the couple arrived in Madrid, where Power was to begin filming *Solomon and Sheba*. They planned some side-trips to Italy and Switzerland during breaks. However, on November 15, Power suffered a massive heart attack similar to his father's while filming a dueling scene

---

[76] Factinate

[77] Factinate

[78] Tyrone Power, King of 20th Century Fox, Deborah Minardos Power – www.tyrone-power.com/biography_debbie.html

with George Sanders. Sanders was admittedly not a good fencer and could not seem to get the scene right. On the 20th take, Power began to tire, then fell to the ground. There was no doctor on the set or nearby, and Power died en route to the hospital. His wife had worried aloud about his health, asking him to slow down, but he ignored her advice. The heart attack has been ascribed to both heredity and heavy smoking, sometimes three to four packs per day.

Power had often said that he only had two wishes: to have a son and to die on stage. On the set, he was "consumed with stress."[79] Heart trouble was part of his genetic line, but Power "didn't want to know"[80] the details of his health. The studio ordered him to undergo a mandatory checkup and wanted to run a cardiogram, but he refused the procedure.

Director King Vidor had asked for Power to lead the film, and by the time of his death, he had finished 75% of the shooting. Power was hurriedly replaced by Yul Brynner, and the film co-starred Gina Lollobrigida. Since Power was one of the finest actor-swordsmen in Hollywood, several long

---

[79] Factinate

[80] Factinate

shots of Power were used and mixed with Brynner. In some of them, Power is still easily recognizable. There was little similarity between the two, so inevitably, the movie gives an uneven impression.

Solomon and Sheba "stumbled"[81] from being "resolutely silly a lot of the time,"[82] and despite the release of *Ben Hur*, the older style of Biblical epics was clearly falling out of favor.

Power was buried at Hollywood Cemetery November 21, 1958, in a full military service. He had remained in the Marine Corps, eventually reaching the rank of major. A memorial service was held at the Chapel of the Psalm with Chaplain Thomas M. Gibson presiding, very near to the tombs of Douglas Fairbanks, Sr. and Douglas Fairbanks, Jr. Pallbearers included Charles Laughton, Raymond Massey, Tommy Noonan, Theodore Richmond, and Murray Steckler. Cesar Romero delivered the eulogy, which was written by George Sanders. Sanders said, "I shall always remember Tyrone Power as a man who gave more of himself than it was wise for him to give, until in

[81] Classic Movie Favorites, August 29, 2015, The Tragic Death of Tyrone Power Before His Time – www.classicmoviefavorites/
[82] Classic Movie Favorites

the end, he gave his life."[83]

The inscription on Power's tomb reads, "Good night, sweet prince."[84] At the gravesite, Laurence Olivier read the poem *High Flight* by American poet John Gillespie Magee, Jr. An added inscription came from *Hamlet*: "There is special providence in the fall of a sparrow. If it be now 'tis not to come. If it be now, yet it will come. The readiness is all."[85] Henry King, who directed Power in 11 films and inspired him to learn to fly, flew over the ceremony. The two had flown together, especially during Power's first experiences aloft.

Power's will stipulated that his eyes were to be donated to the Estelle Doheny Eye Foundation. There is a memorial service at the cemetery every year on November 15, and over half a century later it is still well attended. His last complete work was a Public Service Announcement about heart health, spotting the signs of a heart attack, and the importance of going to the hospital to check it out.

On January 22, 1959, about two months after

---

[83] Tyrone Power, King of 20th Century Fox
[84] Classic Movie Favorites
[85] Classical Movie Favorites

Power's death, Deborah gave birth to the son Power had always wanted. Minardos named him Tyrone William Power IV. Years later, he would carry on the tradition with a baby boy of his own, Tyrone Keenan Power, extending the family's theater legacy for yet another generation. Tyrone IV attended Pomona College and made movies such as *California Casanova*, *Elvis in Paradise*, *Dream Killer*, and *Cocoon*, the last of which was made with Don Ameche.

In 1967, Tyrone Power's likeness appeared on the Beatles' album, *Sgt. Pepper's Lonely Hearts Club Band*. Actor and comedian Wally Cox made a famous reference to Power in an iconic underwear ad: "I may look like Wally Cox, but inside I'm Tyrone Power."[86]

The lead character in a play entitled *Filthy Rich*, a film-noir parody is named Tyrone Power. He is also mentioned in other films, perhaps most notably the legendary *Sunset Boulevard*: "Can you see Ty Power as a shortstop?"[87] In *Flags of Our Fathers*, the character of Rene Gagnon is referred to as

---

[86] IMDB
[87] IMDB

Tyrone Power due to his good looks.

A cartoon artist from Marvel Comics stated that several of his organization's characters are based on older film stars, and Tyrone Power is embodied in the Egyptian magician Ibis the Invincible.

Power has an entire chapter devoted to him in Jeanine Basinger's *The Star Machine* entitled *Disillusioned: Tyrone Power.*

When rumors surfaced suggesting that Power was bi-sexual, those who knew him wondered how he could possibly have had time for that "considering the sheer number of heterosexual amors he had gathered."[88]

In November of 2008, an event was held at the American Cinematheques Egyptian Theatre to mark the 50th anniversary of Power's death. Four films were shown including *Love is News* ('37), *The Mark of Zorro* ('40), *The Razor's Edge* ('46), and *Nightmare Alley* ('47). Attending were Coleen Gray, Piper Laurie, Terry Moore, and Jayne Meadows.

Tyrone IV began work on *Comanche Station* in

[88] Classic Hollywood - #115

2014 and continued with a comedy entitled *The Extra*. Television credits included *Cheers* and the *Bold and the Beautiful*. He says of his father, "We were two hands brushing by each other."[89]

Daughters Taryn and Romina were keeping the Power legacy alive in 2019. Romina has made several films, including Marquis de Sade's *Justine*, *Go Go Tales*, and *Mezzanotte d'Amore*. She is also part of a musical duo Al Bano with ex-husband Albano Carrisi. Taryn Power has appeared in *Sinbad and the Eye of the Tiger*, *The Count of Monte Christo*, and *Maria*.

The Hollywood Museum features several iconic costumes worn by Power in his various films. Prominent among them is the Matador "suit in lights"[90] from *Blood and Sand*, the embroidered pants from *The Mark of Zorro*, the coat from *Son of Fury: The Story of Benjamin Blake*, the black hat with red feathers from *Captain from Castile*, and the navy suit from *Luck of the Irish*. Also included is his silk brocade dressing gown and a number of scripts.

[89] Robyn Flans, American Profile, Where Are They Now: Tyrone Power, March 9, 2014 –
www.americanprofile.com/articles/tyrone-power-jr-where-are-they-now-video
[90] Hollywood Museum, Tyrone Power, 2014 – www.thehollywoodmuseum.com

Power was immortalized in the song *My Baby Just Cares for Me*: "My baby doesn't go for Tyrone Power. She'd rather be with me by the hour."[91] When romance novelist Barbara Cartland was asked how she could be a virgin and still write such steamy novels, she answered, "We didn't need sex. We had Tyrone Power."[92]

If Power's legacy has receded in comparison to other stars of the era, it is likely because during his life, Power had lost out on many choice roles either by rejecting them or being stymied by Zanuck. Zanuck was always furious that Power was given such a short amount of screen time in *Marie Antoinette*, and he constantly refused other loan offers as a result. Such was the case of Paris in *King's Row*, a role that went to Robert Cummings, while *Golden Boy* fell to William Holden after Zanuck turned down the role without consulting Power. Harry Cohn of MGM had always desperately wanted to steal Power away from Zanuck, but once he had the chance, the actor turned down *From Here to Eternity* to go off and tour a

---

[91] IMDB
[92] IMDB

play.

Zanuck also "foolishly"[93] denied the makers of *Gone with the Wind* access to Power, while his role in *How Green Was My Valley* was cut completely. He also turned down the role of the Mexican revolutionary in *Viva Zapata!* Marlon Brando took it instead. During a period of distaste with moviemaking, Power also rejected the role of Robert Browning in *The Barretts of Wimpole Street*, in which he would have starred with Deborah Kerr.

Despite it all, according to Quigley Publishing Co.'s International Motion Picture Almanac, Power was one of the top 100 box office stars of all time, and Fox never lost interest in Power. He lost interest in them, going as far back as the *Nightmare Alley* debacle. *Nightmare Alley* was an immense point of pride, and among his most stinging disappointments. It was as far as he could go away from himself, the most adventurous and vulnerable piece of acting he ever attempted. Power "earns every single tear the viewers have to give. As a wretched outcast from life's banquet, he's as low as a man can go."[94]

---

[93] Not Starring, Tyrone Power – www.notstarring.com/actors/power-tyrone
[94] Sassmouth Dames, Tyrone Power's Reversal of Fortune in Nightmare Alley (1947) – www.sassmouthdames.com/2017/09/10

Perhaps inevitably, Tyrone Power draws constant comparisons to fellow swashbuckler Errol Flynn, and to a lesser degree the Fairbanks family. Flynn and Power appeared together only once, in Hemingway's *The Sun Also Rises*, and the fact that they both made swashbuckler films is their only truly common thread. The far more famous superstar, Flynn "is almost too dynamic for his movies…extravagant vehicles for his outsized talents"[95] as a maker of self-oriented extravaganzas. Power, on the other hand, worked brilliantly within the framework of the story and was highly collaborative. "Less a superman figure…his characters are often subordinate to strong stories. But even when Power's pictures fall short of perfection, they tend to be both intelligent and distinctive."[96]

In David Niven's memoir, entitled *Bring on the Empty Horses*, he referred to Tyrone Power as the "original bad Santa."[97] He might have had the looks, "graceful carriage and easy laughter,"[98] but his

---

[95] tmc.com

[96] tmc.com

[97] Vanity Fair, Old Hollywood's Most Scandalous Secrets, As Told by David Niven – www.vanityfair.com/hollywood/2020/05/david-niven-memoir-scandals-old-hollywood

[98] Vanity Fair

confidence was shattered by performing for children. Playing Santa at a Christmas party for a host of Hollywood children (including a young Candice Bergen), he was nothing short of terrified, "lean[ing] heavily on a bottle of Scotch, soused when he turned up dressed as Father Christmas."[99]m On his way up the lawn, Niven accidentally turned the sprinklers on him, but he sat down anyway with the children of Gary Cooper and Rosalind Russell on his knee, sopping wet. When Santa finally "staggered off, some of the children cried…and one complained about his breath."[100]

Power never received an Oscar for Best Actor, but four of his films were nominated in the category of Best Picture. If such a thing is an oversight, it has happened in numerous cases over the history of the Academy Awards. He failed to land a role in an iconic film such as *Gone with the Wind* or *Casablanca*, though he won one Bambi Award for *The Black Rose*. In 1960, he posthumously received a star on the Walk of Fame, and he was nominated to receive a second Bambi for *The Wonderful Urge*.

---

[99] Vanity Fair

[100] Vanity Fair

Maria Ciaccia, contributing editor and noted interviewer for *Hollywood Magazine*, had the opportunity to sit down with Power before his death, and she claimed that of all the leading men in Hollywood's "golden era," Tyrone Power was her absolute favorite. She pointed out that Power "wasn't the best actor of the bunch – that honor belongs to Gregory Peck. He wasn't the sexiest, either – that honor belongs to Errol Flynn. More than any of them, he came across as genuinely warm, sensitive, and unaffected."[101] As an actor, Ciaccia thoughtfully described him as "versatile, disciplined, hard-working…charismatic…he exuded a great warmth and charm…committed to acting and [was] mindful of his family dynasty.[102] As a man, she cast him as being "extremely passionate, down to Earth, funny [and] generous to a fault, loyal, and non-confrontational – given to some dark moods."[103] He was unhappy about his success being ascribed to mere good looks, "fell in love hard and fast, married in haste, repented at great leisure, and paid a fortune in alimony until the day he died."[104]

---

[101] Altfg.com

[102] Altfg.com

[103] Altfg.com

[104] Altfg.com

Many have concurred that Tyrone Power was more than a great star, despite his skills being frequently overlooked due to his handsome, poised appearance. The subtleties of his acting "grew more impressive with the passage of time."[105] He combined "charm with a bit of the rogue; at the same time, his performance conveyed a thoughtful intelligence. He radiates integrity, yet he was also effective in portraying more troubled – or troubling – characters."[106]

From *The Razor's Edge* through *Nightmare Alley* and *Witness for the Prosecution,* he showed "an admirable desire to improve and stretch as an actor."[107] Just as impressively, he was popular among both fans and coworkers. Fred Lawrence Guiles, in his 1979 biography *Tyrone Power: The Last Idol,* suggests that he was "admired by nearly everyone in the film colony."[108]

Fortunately, the vast majority of Power's films are available on digital media now, and over 60 years after his death, some still find it "hard to wonder

[105] Laura Grieve, Miscellaneous Musings, Classic Flix – www.classicflix.com/bldg/2013/07/22/tyrone-poewr-one-of-the-best

[106] Laura Grieve

[107] Laura Grieve

[108] Laura Grieve

about the great performances that might have been,"[109]

Online Resources

<u>Other books about 20th century history by Charles River Editors</u>

Further Reading

Aliperti, Cliff, Tyrone Power in Son of Fury: The Story of Benjamin Blake (1942), Immortal Ephemera – www.immortalephemera.com

Altfg.com, Linda Christian: First Bond Girl, Tyrone Power Wife and Diego Rivera Model

Archive.org, Lloyd's of London, by Henry King – www.archive.org/1936LloydsofLondon

Bradford, Barry, The Razor's Edge – A Frustrating and Fascinating Film – www.barrybradford.com/razors-edge-frustrating-fascinating-film/

Britannica, The 1940s – www.britannica.com/biography/Edmund-Goulding#ref1177586

---

[109] Laura Grieve

Classic Hollywood #115, Stuff Nobody Cares About, Tyrone Power "No good Reason to get married" – www.stuffnobodycaresabout.com/2021/07/25/classic-hollywood-115-tyrone-power/

Classic Movie Favorites, August 29, 2015, The Tragic Death of Tyrone Power Before His Time – www.classicmoviefavorites/

Factinate, Dashing Facts about Tyrone Power, Hollywood's Doomed Leading Man – www.factinate.com/people/facts-tyrone-power/

Flans, Robyn, American Profile, Where Are They Now: Tyrone Power, March 9, 2014 – www.americanprofile.com/articles/tyrone-power-jr-where-are-they-now-video

Four Star Films, Blood and Sand (1941) – www.fourstarfilms.com2019/03.17/blood-and-sand-1941/

Grieve, Laura, Miscellaneous Musings, Classic Flix – www.classicflix.com/bldg/2013/07/22/tyrone-poewr-one-of-the-best

Hollywood Museum, Tyrone Power, 2014 – www.thehollywoodmuseum.com

IMDB, Tyrone Power, Biography – www.imdb.com

IMDB, The Mississippi Gambler – www.imdb.com/title/tt0046080/reviews/

Lady Eve's Reel Life, Remembering Tyrone Power, Aug. 25, 2012 – www.ladyevesreallife.com/2012/08

Lana Turner.com, Lanta Turner and Tyrone Power – www.lana-turner.com/lana-turner-and-tyrone-power/

Legacy, The Swashbuckling Tyrone Power – www.legacy.com/news/celebrity-deaths/the-swashbuckling-tyrone-power/

Not Starring, Tyrone Power – www.notstarring.com/actors/power-tyrone

NY Times, The 1947 'Nightmare Alley': A Dark View of Class as Destiny – www.nytimes.com2021/12/19/nightmare-alley-1947.html

Sassmouth Dames, Tyrone Power's Reversal of Fortune in Nightmare Alley (1947) – www.sassmouthdames.com/2017/09/10

tcm.com, Alexander's Ragtime Band, 1938 – www.tcm.com/tcmb/title/66978

Theiapolis, The House in the Square – www.theiapolis.com/movie-240N

Tyrone Power, A Brief Biography – www.tyrone-power.com/biography_tv.html

Tyrone Power, King of 20th Century Fox, Deborah Minardos Power – www.tyrone-power.com/biography_debbie.html

Tyrone Power, King of 20th Century Fox – www.tyrone-power.com/lloydsoflondon-story.html

Vanity Fair, Old Hollywood's Most Scandalous Secrets, As Told by David Niven – www.vanityfair.com/hollywood/2020/05/david-niven-memoir-scandals-old-hollywood

Variety Magazine.com, Thin Ice – www.variety.com/film/reviews/thin-ice-1200411309/